MARIA MARTEN OR MURDER IN THE RED BARN

A Melodrama

by Constance Cox

SAMUEL FRENCH

samuelfrench.co.uk

FOR AMATEUR PRODUCTION ENQUIRIES

UNITED KINGDOM AND WORLD
EXCLUDING NORTH AMERICA
plays@samuelfrench.co.uk
020 7255 4302/01

Each title is subject to availability from Samuel French,
depending upon country of performance.

Acting Editions

BORN TO PERFORM

Playscripts designed from the ground up to work the way you do in rehearsal, performance and study

Larger, clearer text for easier reading

Wider margins for notes

Performance features such as character and props lists, sound and lighting cues, and more

+ CHOOSE A SIZE AND STYLE TO SUIT YOU

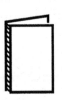

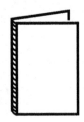

STANDARD EDITION

Our regular paperback book at our regular size

SPIRAL-BOUND EDITION

The same size as the Standard Edition, but with a sturdy, easy-to-fold, easy-to-hold spiral-bound spine

LARGE EDITION

A4 size and spiral bound, with larger text and a blank page for notes opposite every page of text. Perfect for technical and directing use

LEARN MORE | **samuelfrench.co.uk/actingeditions**

**Other plays by CONSTANCE COX
published and licensed by Samuel French**

Because of the Lockwoods

The Bride of Death

A Christmas Carol

The Caliph's Minstrel

The Count of Monte Christo

Everyman

Lady Audley's Secret

Mansfield Park

A Miniature Beggar's Opera

Miss Letitia

The Murder Game

Northanger Abbey

Spring at Marion

Three Knaves of Normandy

A Time for Loving

Trilby

The Vampire

Vanity Fair

The Woman in White

What Brutes Men Are

CHARACTERS

MARIA MARTEN
NANCY MARTEN, *her sister*
SETH ROBINS, *Nancy's sweetheart*
JEMMY HOGAN
MRS MARTEN, *Maria's mother*
MR MARTEN, *Maria's father*
SARAH HERNE, *a gipsy*
BELL ⎱ *gipsies*
ABIGAIL ⎰
MRS CORDER
WILLIAM CORDER, *her son*
DORA MANNERING
JENNY, *a maid*
JASPER RYAN, *a detective*

The scene throughout is a green before the cottage of Mr Marten.

Period: Early nineteenth century. About 1827.

(**Note:** The "mood" music suggested to create atmosphere and
to mark the passage of time is not absolutely essential. It does,
however, help the "feeling" of the piece very much, and was
an integral part of Victorian melodrama. If different music is
preferred, it may, of course, be substituted.)

*This play won the Advanced Cup and the Highest Marks in the
1969 Drama Festival of the Sussex Federation of Townswomen's
Guilds. The Adjudicator was Reginald Campion*

Outside the MARTENS' *cottage. On one side is the trellised entrance to the cottage, and above this an opening leading to the fields and the village. Opposite this opening is another to the high road and orchard. A cut-out bush stands below this opening, and another just above the path to the fields. Below the former bush is a small bench.*

A gay traditional country dance tune is heard, "GALLOPEDE".

When the curtain rises, MARIA, SETH, NANCY *and* JEMMY *are discovered playing Blind Man's Buff.* SETH *is blindfolded, and the others are laughing as they dodge him.*

SETH Got you! *(He grabs* JEMMY.*)*

JEMMY *pushes* SETH *to* MARIA.

Dang you, no, I haven't!

MARIA *turns* SETH *round, then pushes him away. Music fades.*

Hold hard, you be getting me dizzy! *(He moves towards the bench.)*

NANCY *(moving below the bench)* You were born dizzy and brainless, Seth Robins! *(She dances in front of him.)*

SETH *(grabbing her)* Got you! Now, now, no struggling. You keep still while I guess. *(He feels her.)* She's got skirts on, so she be a woman.

MARIA *and* JEMMY *laugh.*

She's got her hair down, so she still be a maid. *(He feels* NANCY's *face.)* She b'aint got a moustache, so she be comely.

NANCY *bites* SETH's *hand.*

Ee, she bit me!

JEMMY *(moving away)* Serve you right for being so rude. Go on, guess who it is.

SETH There's only one lass I know what'd bite the hand of the man who's in love with her, and that's Nan Marten! *(He takes off the blindfold.)*

NANCY You cheat! I believe you could see all the time!

SETH No, I couldn't and I weren't cheating neither. So now I'll have my kiss from you and no more arguing. Come over here! *(He grabs* NANCY *and pulls her on to the bench beside him.)* Now then, me girl, there's that for you! *(He kisses her heartily.)*

MARIA *(clapping her hands)* Well done, Seth!

NANCY And that's for you, Impudence! *(She slaps* SETH's *face and jumps off the bench, moving away.)*

SETH Ee, the way she treats me you'd think we was married already!

NANCY *(advancing to him)* Who says I'm ever going to marry you?

The introductory music starts.

SETH
    I DO, SEE?

NANCY
    AND WHY?

SETH
    'COS YOU'RE IN LOVE WITH ME, MY GIRL. THAT'S WHY.

    SONG: "I LOVES 'EE AND THEE LOVES ME"

    TUNE: "LITTLE BROWN JUG"

I LOVES 'EE AND THEE LOVES ME,
I KNOW THEE DOES SO WED WE'LL BE

NANCY

I THINK THEE'S A SILLY LOUT— *(She moves away.)*
IF 'EE COMES NEAR ME 'EE'LL GET A CLOUT.

SETH

YES, YOU DO.

JEMMY

SAY YOU DO.

MARIA

SISTER DEAR, HE LOVES YOU TRUE.

> **JEMMY** *and* **MARIA** *urge* **NANCY** *towards* **SETH**. *He rises and advances very slowly as he sings.* **NANCY** *backs.*

SETH

ON THE DAY THAT WE GETS WED,
I'LL BUY A GREAT BIG DOUBLE BED!

NANCY You've got to get me first!

> **NANCY** *runs out towards the high road.*

SETH *(following her)* You wait, me girl, till I catches you. I'll have you yet!

> **SETH** *runs out after* **NANCY**.

> **MARIA** *and* **JEMMY** *laugh.*

JEMMY It's a shame how she teases him all the time.

MARIA It's only Nan's fun. She really loves him. She'll make a good wife for him. *(moves to bench)*

JEMMY I know. I envy him with all my heart.

MARIA You envy Seth? That bumpkin!

JEMMY He's marrying the girl he loves. I wish I could say the same.

MARIA Oh, Jemmy, don't!

JEMMY I swear I'd be good to you...

MARIA I know you would – but I don't love you.

JEMMY We've been friends since childhood. You might grow to love me.

MARIA But if I didn't, think how wretched I should make you. And besides, I... *(rises and moves away)*

JEMMY What?

MARIA Nothing.

JEMMY There is something. *(moving to her)* Tell me.

MARIA Jemmy, don't you ever feel you want to leave this place?

JEMMY *(amused)* Leave Polstead? No, why should I? I was born here.

MARIA So was I – but sometimes it stifles me. There's a great big world outside this village, Jemmy, and I know nothing of it. And if I marry you I know I never shall.

JEMMY Maria, I'd do my best to make you happy...

MRS MARTEN *enters from the cottage.*

MRS MARTEN Tea's all ready, children. Why, where have Nan and Seth gone off to?

MARIA They ran towards the orchard, Mother. I'll fetch them.

JEMMY No, I'll go.

MRS MARTEN Thank you, Jemmy. Then come back and have tea with us.

JEMMY Thank you, Mrs Marten.

JEMMY *exits after* NAN *and* SETH. MRS MARTEN *goes into the cottage.*

MARIA *(moving to the bench)* Poor Jemmy. I know he loves me truly, and perhaps if I were wise I'd say yes to him. But there is something in my heart that tells me he is not the man that I was meant for. *(She sits on the bench.)*

SARAH HERNE, *a sultry, middle-aged gipsy, enters from the fields and stands watching* **MARIA.**

I feel so strongly there is someone waiting – someone who is different from the village lads I've always known – who'll take me away from this quiet place, and into a life that's gay and bright and full of wonder.

SARAH *chuckles.*

(starting and looking round) Who's there?

SARAH *(coming down)* Only me, pretty lady. Forgive me if I startled you.

MARIA *(rising)* What do you want?

SARAH A morsel of food of your charity, my dear. I've walked far today, and I'm very tired.

MARIA Poor soul. Sit you down on this bench – *(Taking* **SARAH** *to the bench)* – and I'll fetch you something.

SARAH Bless you, pretty one.

The introductory music starts.

MARIA *goes into the cottage.*

SARAH *looks furtively round, then sits on the bench.*

SONG: "MY SISTER"

TUNE: "OH, THE OAK AND THE ASH"

MY SISTER WAS KIND AND GENTLE AND GAY,
HER LIFE IT WAS HAPPY, WITH NAUGHT TO DISMAY.
TILL CORDER DID MEET HER, OH SAD DAY TO PROVE,
FOR SHE LISTENED WHILST HE SPOKE HIS FALSE WORDS OF
    LOVE.

HE RUINED HER LIFE THEN CAST HER ASIDE,
HER HEART IT WAS BROKEN AND LONELY SHE DIED.
I CAME TO HER DEATH-BED WHEN LIFE IT WAS FLED,
AND I LAID HER TO REST IN HER LAST EARTHLY BED.

SARAH *rises.*

MY VOW IT WAS MADE AS I KNELT BY HER SIDE,
I WOULD HUNT HER BETRAYER WHATE'ER MIGHT BETIDE,
WHEREE'ER HE MIGHT GO OR MY FOOTSTEPS BE LED,
I NEVER WOULD REST UNTIL CORDER WAS DEAD!
WHEREE'ER HE MIGHT GO OR MY FOOTSTEPS BE LED,
    (repeat)
I NEVER WOULD REST UNTIL CORDER WAS DEAD!

SARAH *moves down and addresses the audience.*

Here I am at last in the village of Polstead, where my poor young sister died of a broken heart, betrayed and discarded by a villain and a seducer! But I have sworn vengeance upon him, and if this young girl is heart-free, I will use her as my weapon. I heard enough to tell me she is discontented with her life here. I will foster her ambitions, and through her send that villain to the scaffold! But hush, she comes! *(She sits on the bench.)*

MARIA *enters with a bundle of food.*

MARIA Here is some bread and cheese for you to carry with you.

SARAH *(rising)* Your heart is as kind as your face is pretty, my dear. What can I do to repay you? *(She puts the bundle on the bench.)*

MARIA Nothing. I give it to you gladly.

SARAH Ah, but Sarah Herne does not take something for nothing. I am poor, but proud, my dear. Show me your hand.

MARIA My hand? But why?

SARAH That I may read your future for you.

MARIA My future! *(moving away)* No!

SARAH *(following her)* Wouldn't you like to hear what lies in store for you?

MARIA I am afraid.

SARAH Of what? Come, let me see it. *(She takes MARIA's hand and draws her to the bench.)* Don't be nervous, pretty lady. Sit you here beside me.

SARAH *and* MARIA *sit on the bench.*

Why, this is a most lucky hand!

MARIA Lucky?

SARAH I see love and admiration – ah – and riches!

MARIA Riches? No, that can't be! You're mistaken!

SARAH 'Tis all written in your hand, my dear. Soon – very soon – you'll meet a rich and handsome gentleman.

MARIA *(aside)* It's all I ever hoped for! *(to SARAH)* Will he fall in love with me?

SARAH Indeed he will.

MARIA And marry me?

SARAH *And* marry you. Did I not say it was a lucky hand?

MARIA *(rising and moving away)* I can scarcely believe it. Do you tell me true?

SARAH *(rising and picking up her bundle)* I tell you true, my dear. So keep your heart free for him. Now I must be on my way.

MARIA Goodbye, and thank you.

SARAH Bless you, my pretty, and remember what the gipsy said.

SARAH *chuckles and exits to the high road.*

MARIA *(moving to the bench and sitting)* Rich and handsome – and he'll fall in love with me! And I shall marry him! Oh, how my heart flutters! *(She sits looking at her hand.)*

SETH *enters from the high road followed by* JEMMY *and* NANCY.

SETH *(as he enters, to* JEMMY*)* What did you have to come and interrupt us for? She were just on the point of saying yes to me.

NANCY I was just on the point of slapping your face again, you great oaf! *(She sees* MARIA.*)* Why, Maria, what's the matter? *(She sits beside* MARIA.*)* You look all bemused.

MARIA A woman was here just now – a gipsy...

JEMMY Did she frighten you? You look so pale.

MARIA Frighten me – no! She made me very happy.

MRS MARTEN *enters from the cottage.*

MRS MARTEN Are you young people never coming in to tea?

SETH I'm coming now. I be right starved.

MRS MARTEN *smiles and goes back into the cottage.*

(grabbing NANCY's *hand and pulling her up)* And come you in as well. I wants to feed you up before I marries 'ee.

SETH *and* NANCY *exit into the cottage.*

JEMMY Maria, what is it? What did that gipsy say to you?

MARIA *(rising)* Nothing I can tell you, Jemmy.

JEMMY Maria, you must. It's changed you somehow.

MARIA No, Jemmy, no!

JEMMY But, Maria...

MARIA Oh, leave me alone! Please leave me alone!

MARIA *runs off towards the high road.*

JEMMY *moves a few paces after her, then turns and moves down to the audience. Music starts softly, and continues*

as he speaks – the minuet from Handel's "BERENICE".
Eight bars.

JEMMY

WHAT'S HAPPENED SINCE I LEFT HER, SHE HAS CHANGED.
SHE NEVER USED ME THUS BEFORE, THO' VOWS WE'D NOT
   EXCHANGED.
I'VE LOVED HER TRUE FOR MANY A DAY, AND STILL I'LL
   PERSEVERE,
WITH CONSTANT HEART AND TENDER LOVE, I'LL HOPE TO
   WIN MY DEAR.

With a look in the direction **MARIA,** *who has gone,*
JEMMY *exits into the cottage.*

The music swells to mark the passage of time – a further
eight bars.

MARTEN *enters from the high road, carrying a bundle*
of wood.

The music fades as he speaks.

MARTEN Wife, wife, be you at home?

MRS MARTEN *enters from the cottage, wiping her hands*
on her apron.

MRS MARTEN Ay, husband, here I am. What be the matter?

MARTEN Here's Mrs Corder and her son a-coming to our cottage!

MRS MARTEN The squire and his mother? Nay, but, husband,
you're mistaken surely?

MARTEN I tell 'ee, wife, they're coming up the path. And here
they be!

MRS CORDER *and* **WILLIAM CORDER** *enter from the high*
road. **MRS CORDER** *is an aristocratic lady.* **WILLIAM**
is an extremely handsome, clean-shaven young man.

Make thy curtsy, wife!

MRS MARTEN *curtsies to* **MRS CORDER**.

Good mornin' to 'ee, ma'am – and to 'ee, squire.

MRS CORDER Good morning to you, Marten—Mrs Marten.

WILLIAM *nods to the* **MARTENS** *then moves below the bench, taking out a snuff-box.*

MRS MARTEN Our humble home be honoured, ma'am. How may we serve you?

MRS CORDER I'm told you make most excellent lace, Mrs Marten, and would like to see some. Have you any you can show me?

MRS MARTEN That I have, ma'am. I've been making some against my daughter's wedding.

WILLIAM *(suddenly)* Your daughter's wedding?

MRS MARTEN That's right, sir. She's being wed within the month.

WILLIAM *(over casually)* Which daughter is that? You have two, I believe?

MRS MARTEN My daugher Nancy, sir, to young Seth Robins.

WILLIAM *(aside)* All's well, I find. It's not the one I've cast my eyes upon.

MRS CORDER Why, do you know the girl in question, William?

WILLIAM I may have seen her in the village, Mother. Aren't you going in to see the lace?

MRS MARTEN Pray step inside our cottage, ma'am. Husband, set out the cowslip wine for Mrs Corder.

MARTEN *goes into the cottage.*

MRS CORDER William, are you coming in as well?

WILLIAM No, Mother, I'll wait here for you.

MRS CORDER I'll not be long.

MRS CORDER *goes into the cottage.*

MRS MARTEN *(to* WILLIAM*)* Shall Marten bring you out a glass of cowslip wine, sir?

WILLIAM Thank you, no. Don't bother.

Dropping a curtsy, MRS MARTEN *goes into the cottage.*

(to the audience) What a lucky chance it was my mother thought to purchase lace of Mrs Marten. It may open a way for me to meet her daughter, Maria. For many a day I've had designs upon her. She's as pretty as a picture and she fires my blood and I'm determined I will have her. *(moving up stage)* I saw her in the orchard as we walked towards the cottage. *(smiling)* Shall I go and meet her accidentally? *(He looks off towards the high road.)* No – happy fortune – here she comes!

MARIA *enters quickly from the high road, carrying a basket of apples. She is looking back over her shoulder, and does not see* WILLIAM *until she nearly runs into him.*

WILLIAM Why so hasty, pretty maiden?

MARIA *(turning)* Oh – oh, sir! *(She curtsies.)*

WILLIAM Another second and you would have run into my arms.

MARIA Oh, sir, I beg your pardon. I wasn't looking. I –I was running away from Jemmy Hogan.

WILLIAM And who is Jemmy Hogan, pray, that you should run away from him?

MARIA *(bashfully)* He wants to be – my sweetheart, sir.

WILLIAM Does he, indeed? *(looking at her)* I must admit that Jemmy Hogan has good taste.

MARIA Please, sir, you mustn't flatter me. *(moving towards the cottage)*

WILLIAM I speak the truth. In fact, I'd willingly be Jemmy Hogan's rival. *(He moves close to her.)*

MARIA *(moving away)* You, sir? Oh, no, you jest!

WILLIAM *(following her)* I myself, my sweet Maria. I've seen you often – though perhaps you've not seen me.

MARIA *(looking down)* Yes, sir, I have.

WILLIAM And wished as many times that I might speak with you and tell you of my love.

MARIA Your love! *(She looks at him.)* You mean – your love for *me*?

WILLIAM My love for you. *(He takes her hand.)* May I – dare I hope that you return my passion? Speak, dear Maria, and tell me that I do not love in vain.

MARIA *(moving to the bench)* But, sir, I'm far beneath you. What could you want with me – a poor man's daughter? *(She sits)*

WILLIAM I want the favour of your heart and hand. I wish to marry you, Maria.

MARIA *places the basket by the side of the bench.*

MARIA To marry me!

WILLIAM *(kneeling by the bench)* Will you, Maria? Will you become my wife?

MARIA It would be all I ever longed for! Oh, what happiness! And would you take me away from here – perhaps to London?

WILLIAM *(rising and sitting beside her; with a smile)* You shall go anywhere your heart desires. Only say yes to me.

MARIA Yes, oh yes, dear William!

WILLIAM Sweet Maria! *(He kisses her hand.)*

MARIA When shall we tell my parents? Shall we tell them now?

WILLIAM *(rising)* No, not yet. *(He moves away.)*

MARIA *(rising)* But if you wish to marry me...

WILLIAM *(turning to her)* We must delay our marriage for a while. My mother will be against it.

SARAH *appears in the entrance from the fields and stands watching.*

MARIA Then we must part?

WILLIAM No, we shall not part. I'll find a place for you to live, and come and visit you. Then in a month or two, I will produce you as my chosen bride.

MARIA Oh, my love – my dearest! *(She lays her head on his hand.)*

SARAH *withdraws.*

WILLIAM *(to the audience; over* MARIA's *head)* It's done. I have her. *(to* MARIA, *moving away)* Now I must go back to the carriage. My mother must not see us together.

MARIA When shall I hear from you?

WILLIAM Within a day or two, I promise.

WILLIAM *kisses his hand to* MARIA *and exits to the high road.*

MARIA *runs up to watch him off, and waves, then moves downstage.*

MARIA To think that I am loved by such a splendid gentleman! It is all happening as the gipsy said. *(moving to the cottage)* Oh, I have never been so happy as I am today!

MARIA *exits into the cottage.*

SARAH *enters and moves downstage.*

SARAH My scheme begins to work! The seed I planted in her mind has blossomed. The little fool!

BELLE *and* ABIGAIL, *two gipsies, enter from the fields and listen.*

Soon he will grow tired of her and use foul means to cast her off, and then the law will have him! *(She raises her arms.)* Gipsy sister, vengeance is at hand!

BELLE Sarah, we overheard you. What are you doing?

ABIGAIL You have a dreadful plan to use that girl. We know it!

SARAH I am avenging our sister, who was betrayed by William Corder. Leave me alone!

ABIGAIL But this village girl was not to blame. Why should she suffer?

SARAH She is a pawn in my game. I care nothing for her.

BELLE But we do. She has been kind to our tribe. I tell you, Sarah, I shall warn her.

SARAH Try, if you like! You'll find she will not listen to you.

MARIA *appears at the cottage door.*

Good morning, pretty lady. Happy fortune go with you.

MARIA *(smiling)* I think it does, good gipsy.

SARAH *exits towards the fields.*

ABIGAIL Lady, may we speak with you? It is important.

BELLE Indeed it is.

MARIA *(moving between them)* What do you wish to say to me?

BELLE Lady, you are deceived by William Corder.

MARIA What?

ABIGAIL Though he speaks you fair, he wants you but to ruin you.

MARIA *(moving to pick up the apple basket)* What wickedness is this? How dare you lie about him?

ABIGAIL It is not lying, lady, but the truth! You must take heed of us!

MARIA I will not hear a word against him! William Corder loves me!

The introductory music starts.

BELLE William Corder is in love with no one but himself!

ABIGAIL Oh, lady, listen!

SONG: "THE GIPSIES' WARNING" - Duet

ABIGAIL AND BELLE

DO NOT TRUST HIM, GENTLE MAIDEN, THOUGH HIS VOICE BE
LOW AND SWEET,
HEED NOT HIM WHO KNELT BEFORE THEE, GENTLY
PLEADING AT THY FEET.
NOW THY LIFE IS AT ITS DAWNING, HEED THOU THEN THY
HAPPY LOT.

MARIA *goes to the cottage door. The gipsies follow.*

LISTEN TO THE GIPSIES' WARNING, GENTLE LADY, TRUST HIM
NOT.
LISTEN TO THE GIPSIES' WARNING, GENTLE LADY, TRUST HIM
NOT.

MARIA Begone, your words are unavailing! Nothing can tear me from him!

MARIA *exits into the cottage.*

ABIGAIL It is useless. She will not listen.

BELLE No, she is bent upon her own destruction.

SARAH *enters from the fields.*

SARAH Did I not say so? Get back to the camp!

ABIGAIL *(pleadingly)* Sarah...

SARAH Do as I say!

Music starts softly. Schumann's "COMING WOE". Eight bars.

BELLE *and* **ABIGAIL** *exit to the fields.*

SARAH *moves downstage, raising her arms, and speaking over the music.*

SARAH

> SISTER IN HEAVEN WHOSE GENTLE HEART WAS BY THIS
>   VILLAIN TORN,
> REVENGE IS NEAR, HE'LL RUE THE DAY HE TREATED YOU
>   WITH SCORN.
> FOR BY MY WILES, THIS GIRL HE'S FALSELY PROMISED HE
>   WILL WED,
> SHALL LEAD HIM STEP BY STEP TOWARDS THE GALLOWS HE
>   SHALL TREAD!

SARAH *laughs wildly and exits to the fields, as the music continues for a further five bars, during which* **MARTEN** *and* **MRS MARTEN** *enter from the cottage. He carries a bundle. She wears a bonnet and cloak and is weeping. Music fades.*

MRS MARTEN Oh, Jonathan, it's hard to leave our cottage. Humble though it is, it's been our home for nigh on forty years.

MARTEN Ah, wife, 'tis hard, but Mrs Corder bids us go, and we've no choice but to obey. We'll find another home, my dear, don't worry.

MRS MARTEN If only we could find Maria I'd be happy. 'Tis twelve months since she ran away from us, and not a word from her.

MRS CORDER *enters from the fields.*

MRS CORDER What, Marten, not gone yet? Did not my bailiff tell you you must leave this property by twelve o'clock?

MRS MARTEN Oh, Mrs Corder, ma'am, why must we go at all? We've been good tenants. Never a penny have we ever owed you all these years.

JEMMY *enters from the cottage, carrying a bundle.*

MRS CORDER My son's wife will require the cottage for her servants. That is reason enough.

MARTEN Be Mr Corder getting married, ma'am?

MRS CORDER Within the month. Now please, be on your way.

MRS CORDER exits to the high road.

SETH and NANCY come out of the cottage carrying baskets or bundles.

NANCY We've got your bundles, Mother. Now there's no need to cry again. *(She leads MRS MARTEN to the bench.)*

NANCY and MRS MARTEN sit together on the bench.

You know you're going to stay with Seth and me until you find another place to go.

JEMMY *(to MARTEN)* Did I hear Mrs Corder say her son was getting married?

MARTEN Ay, Jemmy, you did.

JEMMY But he's no right to wed with any but Maria!

MRS MARTEN Jemmy, what do you mean?

JEMMY He stole Maria away from me. I know he did!

SETH Nay, that proves nothing.

JEMMY Not by itself, it's true. But, as you know, I loved Maria. After she jilted me, I used to follow her in secret. I saw William Corder meet her in the woods, not once, but many times before she disappeared.

NANCY You think he may have wed her, Jemmy?

JEMMY I think he may have promised to, to make her go away with him. And now he means to throw her off to wed this other woman.

MRS MARTEN *(rising and moving to MARTEN)* Oh, poor Maria, what will become of her? Husband, you know I told you of my dreadful dream about her!

MARTEN (*putting his arm round* MRS MARTEN) Nay, nay, don't think of it. (*leading her towards the exit to the high road*) Put trust in heaven and all may yet be well.

MARTEN *and* MRS MARTEN *exit to the high road.*

JEMMY I'll trust in no one but myself! I'll find that villain out and punish him!

SETH Don't 'ee be foolish. Injure William Corder and you'll only harm yourself. Come, Nance, we'll see your parents stowed in comfort, then I must be off to work.

SETH *exits to the high road.* NANCY *rises and follows him.*

JEMMY (*moving downstage; to the audience*) He's right. There's little I can do to make a man like Corder pay. The gentry have their laws, and we, the common folk, obey.

The introductory music of **"HEARTS AND FLOWERS"** *begins.*

YET BY THIS HAND, MY LIFE AND HEART, STILL TO MY LOVE
   SO TRUE,
I SWEAR BEFORE MY END IS COME, CORDER HIS DEEDS SHALL
   RUE.

JEMMY *exits to the high road.*

The music swells.

MARIA *enters from the fields, carrying a baby. She moves slowly to the bench and sits, putting the baby down beside her.*

The music fades.

MARIA Oh, I am so weary! I must sit down before I go and see my parents. What will they say to me? A ruined daughter with an ailing child? Perhaps they'll not be hard on me. I was deceived and foolish, but not wicked.

Voices are heard off towards the high road.

But who comes here?

WILLIAM *enters, smiling into the face of* DORA MANNERING, *a pretty, fashionably dressed girl, who is on his arm. They are followed by* JENNY, *a maid. They stop up centre,* WILLIAM *pointing towards the fields.*

MARIA It's William! He forbade me to return here! I must not let him see me! *(She pulls her shawl over her head and sits with her back to the others.)*

WILLIAM Look yonder, dearest. There you can see the church where we'll be married.

MARIA *(aside)* Married!

DORA Oh, how pretty it is, William! *(moves left, looking off)*

WILLIAM Pretty for a pretty bride. *(He takes her hand.)* How I long for the day to come when I can call you mine.

DORA And will you love me always, William?

WILLIAM Always, my dearest Dora. You will find in me the faithfullest of husbands.

MARIA *(aside)* Ah, wretched me!

DORA And you have never loved another woman? *(moving downstage)*

WILLIAM Never, upon my honour. *(Following her)*

MARIA *(aside)* I can stand no more! *(She rises, throws back her shawl, and turns.)* You lie, William Corder, you lie! Look upon me, then talk about your honour!

WILLIAM *(aside)* The devil – Maria! *(To* DORA*)* Dora, go back to the house and await me there.

DORA But who is this?

WILLIAM A beggar woman who plagues me. Jenny, tell them to bring the carriage to the path. Go quickly!

JENNY Yes, sir. Will you come with me, madam?

DORA No! William, I want to know...

WILLIAM *(passing her towards the high road exit)* Please, my beloved, do as I say.

JENNY Come, madam, this is no place for you.

> **DORA** *exits to the high road, looking curiously at* **MARIA**. **JENNY** *follows her off.*

WILLIAM *(to* **MARIA***; angrily)* What are you doing in this village? Didn't I tell you never to come here again?

MARIA William, our child was ill! You left me penniless.

WILLIAM I would have come, I promise you... *(moving away)*

MARIA No, you meant to desert me! Did I not hear your plans to marry that woman? You, who swore to marry *me* and love me always! Oh, wicked, vile seducer! *(moving to him)*

WILLIAM Maria, be calm. I shall keep my promise to you.

MARIA How can you? Do you mean to wed us both? *(turning away)*

WILLIAM I'm wedding you and you alone, my darling. That other was a scheme that I was forced to by my mother. I had debts, my love. Miss Mannering is an heiress. But now the deeds are signed – the money's in my hands – and you and I can fly to foreign lands together!

As he speaks, he leads her to the bench.

MARIA Oh, William, are you speaking truthfully? Can I believe you? Tell me, I beg of you!

WILLIAM You may believe me, sweetheart. *(moving behind the bench)* How is the child?

MARIA *(sitting on the bench)* Oh, William, it is very ill. See how quiet and pale it lies. *(She picks the baby up gently, then looks at it in horror.)* William, it is not breathing! It is dead! Our little one is dead! *(She weeps.)*

WILLIAM Hush, my beloved, be comforted. Sad though it is, without the child we shall travel faster and safer.

MARIA I loved it so. Oh, William, you must never leave me more, now I have lost it.

WILLIAM Never shall my love be wanting. *(He helps her to rise.)* Go now, and await my coming. *(takes her to centre)*

MARIA Where shall I wait?

WILLIAM At the Red Barn, sweetheart.

MARIA Not the Red Barn! It is so lonely there. It frightens me!

WILLIAM I shall be there within a quarter of an hour. Be brave, Maria. Think of what lies in store for us.

MARIA I will. Oh, William, I was so sad, but now I am so happy. Do not be long, my loved one.

MARIA, *her hand lingering in his, exits towards the high road.*

WILLIAM *watches her out, with a smile on his face. Then he moves angrily downstage.*

WILLIAM *(to the audience)* Wretched girl, she has sealed her own doom by following me back here. Now I must dispose of her, or all will be lost. *(He slaps his pocket.)* Fortunately I have my pistol with me. But her body? It must be buried and that of the child. But how? What's to be done?

SETH *is heard off, from the high road, singing "I LOVES 'EE".*

Who comes here? *(He looks off towards the high road.)* A lucky chance! A yokel with the very tool I require!

SETH *enters with a spade over his shoulder. He pauses to pick his teeth with a straw.*

Hey, my fine fellow!

SETH *looks over his shoulder, then at* WILLIAM.

SETH Who be 'ee talking to?

WILLIAM You, my good man. How would you care to earn a guinea?

SETH No, thanks.

WILLIAM What?

SETH I be finished me work for today. I don't want to work any more.

WILLIAM Fool!

SETH *(belligerently)* What's that?

WILLIAM I mean – how sensible. But the fact is, my good man, I don't wish you to work for the money. I intend to give it to you.

SETH Give it to me? A guinea?

WILLIAM Yes.

SETH *(to the audience)* Well, dang me buttons, and he called I a fool!

WILLIAM Ah, but I want something for it. The loan of your spade for an hour.

SETH Me spade?

WILLIAM Your spade.

SETH And what d'you need me spade for? Be you going to bury something?

WILLIAM *(laughing)* Ha, ha!

SETH *(imitating him)* Ha, ha!

WILLIAM Well, to be perfectly frank, I am. A mad dog that I shot this morning.

SETH I never heerd no shot this morning.

WILLIAM It was near the Red Barn where I shall bury the dog.

SETH Let's see thy guinea.

WILLIAM Here.

WILLIAM *hands* **SETH** *a guinea.* **SETH** *bites it.*

SETH And here be spade. Where will 'ee leave it?

WILLIAM By the barn. You can fetch it tomorrow. Well, good day to you, my man – and thank you.

WILLIAM *exits towards the high road.*

SETH And thank 'ee, sir. *(to the audience)* Well, I'll be danged. A guinea for the loan of me old spade. A few more like him, and I'd never have to work at all. *(chord)*

SONG: *to the tune of "THE MILLER OF DEE"*

IF I HAD GUINEAS EVERY DAY,
OH, WHAT A CHANGE THERE'D BE.
I'D LIVE IN COMFORT, SO I WOULD,
I'D HAVE SPRATS FOR ME TEA.
I'D NEVER DIG NOR CHOP NO WOOD,
'TIS LIKE A LORD I'D BE-E.
AND IF ME WIFE SAID: "GET TO WORK",
I'D SAY: "DON'T TALK TO ME!"

He does a little dance for four bars.

NOW NANCY IS A FINE YOUNG LASS,
AND WED TO HER I BE, *(SITTING ON THE BENCH)*
BUT IF SHE WERE TO TALK LIKE THAT,
I'D SHOW HER WHO I BE.

NANCY *enters from the high road and stands watching him.*

I'D SAY: "NOW, WIFE, YOU KEEP YOUR PLACE,
"AND COOK AND SEW FOR ME-E.
"I BE THE MASTER IN MY HOUSE,
"AND NONE SHALL BULLY ME".

NANCY *comes down to the bench, singing. Repeat of last eight bars.*

NANCY

> AND WHAT WAS THAT I OVERHEARD,
> WHAT WOULD YOU SAY TO ME-E?
> YOU'LL COME BACK HOME AT ONCE, ME LAD,
> OR ELSE I'LL DO FOR 'EE.

NANCY takes SETH by the ear and drags him off to the fields.

*The music changes to Rachmaninoff's **"PRELUDE IN C SHARP MINOR"** beginning at the Agitato.*

On the thirteenth bar of the music, MRS MARTEN is heard calling from the high road entrance, "MARIA, MARIA!" She enters, still calling, and moves downstage.

The music diminishes.

MRS MARTEN Maria! Oh, my child!

MARTEN enters from the high road and runs to MRS MARTEN.

MARTEN Wife, wife, come back! This is madness!

MRS MARTEN *(clinging to him)* She's not here! She's not here!

The music stops.

JEMMY enters from the high road.

JEMMY What be the matter, Mrs Marten?

MRS MARTEN My dream. It came to me again – the seventh time this month. I saw Maria standing here – *(She moves below the bench.)* a baby in her arms. And on her dress there was a great red spreading stain. Oh, Jemmy, I am sure that harm has come to her! *(She sits on the bench.)*

JEMMY So am I. And because of my fears, I've been to London and secured the services of this gentleman.

JASPER RYAN enters from the high road.

MARTEN Who are you, sir? *(standing down left)*

JASPER I am Jasper Ryan, a Bow Street officer. I understand there is some mystery attaching to the disappearance of your daughter.

JEMMY Mystery – and suspicion.

JASPER Whose suspicion?

JEMMY Mine!

SETH *and* **NANCY** *enter from the fields.*

SETH Here, what be going on?

SETH *and* **NANCY** *move to* **MARTEN**, *who talks to them in dumb show.*

JEMMY William Corder wooed Maria. Then he persuaded her to leave her home for him.

NANCY You can't prove that, Jemmy.

JEMMY I can. I have witnesses. *(He moves upstage and beckons off towards the entrance to the fields.)* Come here, both of you.

BELLE *and* **ABIGAIL** *enter.*

JEMMY Did you see William Corder make love to Maria Marten?

ABIGAIL Yes, we did.

BELLE We told her not to trust him, but she wouldn't listen to us.

JEMMY *(to* **JASPER***)* Later, he announced his marriage to an heiress. That were the day, Seth, that he borrowed your spade.

SETH Ay, that he did.

JASPER A spade? Why should he need a spade?

SETH To bury a mad dog, he told me. He give me a guinea for the loan of un.

JASPER Where did he bury it? *(crossing to* **SETH***)*

SETH At the Red Barn, so he said.

JASPER You men, come with me. *(to* **JEMMY***)* We shall need tools. Can you get them?

JEMMY At my house on the way. Come on!

> **JEMMY, JASPER, SETH** *and* **MARTEN** *exit to the high road.* **SARAH** *enters from the fields.*

MRS MARTEN The Red Barn! She was so frightened of that place!

SARAH She did well to be frightened of it. It was an ill place for her. *(moving downstage)*

MRS MARTEN Who are you?

SARAH The sister of a gipsy girl – treated by William Corder as he treated your daughter!

NANCY What do you mean?

SARAH I mean that she is dead – slain by his hand!

> **MRS MARTEN** *gives a cry, and covers her face.* **NANCY** *runs and comforts her, sitting by her on the bench.*
>
> **WILLIAM CORDER** *enters from the high road with* **DORA** *on his arm. They move to centre.*

(pointing at **WILLIAM***)* And here he is, the wretch himself! William Corder, retribution is at hand!

> **WILLIAM** *looks round. The gipsies surround him.* **SARAH** *draws a dagger.*

Seek not to fly! Though we are but women, we will hold you with our lives!

WILLIAM You're mad! Let me pass – let me pass!

DORA William, what is it?

SARAH Let the woman go! She has not harmed us. *(to* **DORA***)* Get you back to your fine house, girl, and enjoy it while you can!

SARAH *pushes* DORA *roughly off towards the fields. At the same moment* SETH *enters from the high road with a shawl.*

SETH Mrs Marten, do you recognise this shawl? *(behind bench)*

MRS MARTEN It's hers – Maria's! Where did you find it?

SETH It were lying in her grave, Mrs Marten – where *he* – *(pointing at* WILLIAM*)* did bury her!

JASPER *and* JEMMY *enter from the high road.*

WILLIAM It's a lie! No matter what you find you have no proof I killed her.

JASPER You deny you killed her, then? *(stands centre)*

WILLIAM Yes, I do! What if she does lie buried in the old Red Barn?

SARAH *laughs triumphantly, standing down left.*

Why do you laugh like that? What have I said?

SARAH You have uttered your own condemnation, William Corder! Nobody told you where Maria's body was found. How did you know it was the old Red Barn?

JASPER *(producing a pistol)* And what of this?

WILLIAM This is not mine!

JASPER No? Yet it has your name upon it.

JEMMY Confess and beg for mercy, Corder! Your hour has come!

CORDER *looks round at the hostile faces, slowly, then he drops to his knees.*

WILLIAM I confess it – I confess it! I did kill her!

SARAH Ah!

WILLIAM Do with me what you will. My life has not been happy since.

JASPER The law will take its course. There'll be no mercy.

SARAH And my sister is avenged! Sister, behold, you shall have blood for blood!

SARAH *strikes her clenched fist on her heart.* **BELLE** *and* **ABIGAIL** *do the same.* **JASPER** *moves to left of* **WILLIAM**.

JASPER *(laying his hand on* **WILLIAM***'s shoulder)* William Corder, have you anything to say before you're taken from this place?

WILLIAM Nothing but this... *(He rises.)*

The music of **"HEARTS AND FLOWERS"** *sounds softly under* **WILLIAM***'s speech.*

FORGIVE MY MISDEEDS, ALL OF YOU,
MY LIFE IS NEAR ITS END.
I LOVED MARIA DEEP AND TRUE,
BUT I MUST MAKE AMEND.
FOR I WAS LED ASTRAY BY GOLD,

To the audience.

AND ALL THE WORLD HOLDS GOOD.
FOR THAT I THREW AWAY TRUE LOVE,
FOR THAT I SHED MY BLOOD.

WILLIAM *kneels, facing slightly up stage. The music changes to the introduction of* **"COCKLES AND MUSSELS"** *as three groups are formed:* **MRS MARTEN, NANCY, SETH** *and* **JEMMY** *right;* **JASPER,** *by* **WILLIAM,** *making the centre group;* **SARAH, BELLE** *and* **ABIGAIL** *left.*

SONG: *to the tune of* **"COCKLES AND MUSSELS"**

THE COMPANY
SO THEY HANGED WILLIAM CORDER,
THEY HANGED WILLIAM CORDER,
THEY HANGED HIM UP HIGH
ON A TALL GALLOWS TREE.

MARIA *enters, dressed as an angel. She stands above* **WILLIAM,** *looking down at him.*

FOR HE MURDERED HIS SWEETHEART,
THE GIRL WHO HAD LOVED HIM,
AND PROMISED HER FALSELY
HIS WIFE SHE SHOULD BE.

WILLIAM *looks up and sees* **MARIA.** *He places his hands together as if praying her for forgiveness.*

Chorus:
A FALSE LOVER'S PROMISE,
A FALSE LOVER'S PROMISE,
HE PROMISED HER FALSELY
HIS WIFE SHE SHOULD BE.

The rest of the **COMPANY** *enters.* **DORA** *joins the group left,* **MRS CORDER, MARTEN** *and* **JENNY** *take their places by the group right.*

WILLIAM *rises and stands beside* **MARIA.**

SO ALL YOU YOUNG PEOPLE,
TAKE HEED OF THIS STORY,
DON'T TRIFLE WITH HEARTS
OR YOU MAY END THE SAME.
BE TRUE TO YOUR LOVER,
DON'T THINK OF ANOTHER,
AND LIFE WILL BE PLEASANT
AND FREE FROM ALL PAIN.

All the **COMPANY** *step forward.*

Chorus:
YES, LIFE WILL BE PLEASANT,
OH, LIFE WILL BE PLEASANT,
THEN LIFE WILL BE PLEASANT,
AND FREE FROM ALL PAIN.

Curtain.

MUSIC PLOT

DETAILS OF SONGS AND SUGGESTED MOOD MUSIC

©"Gallopede" (traditional), Country Dance Tune, Set 1.
Arranged by Cecil Sharp. Published: Novello

"Little Brown Jug" (traditional)

"Oh, the Oak and the Ash" (National Song Book)

"Minuet". Handel from the opera *Berenice*

©"The Gipsies' Warning" (Old Time Popular songs)
Published: Paxton

©"Schumann's "Coming Woe". Opus 124 Album Leaves,
No. 2

©"Hearts and Flowers". Published: Paxton (piano score)

"Miller of Dee" (National Song Book)

©"Prelude in C Sharp Minor", Rachmaninolf (start from
the Agitato)

"Cockles and Mussels" (Irish traditional song)

Permission to perform this play does not include permission
to use any music. Whenever copyright music, or a copyright
arrangement of music is used, a return must be made to the
Performing Right Society. Many halls and theatres are covered
by a PRS licence. In other cases application should be made to
the Society at 29/33 Berners Street, London W1P 4AA.

FURNITURE AND PROPERTY LIST

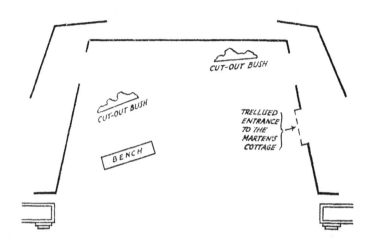

Onstage: Bench
             Two cut-out bushes

Offstage: Bundle of bread and cheese (**Maria**)
             Bundle of wood (**Marten**)
             Basket of apples (**Maria**)
             Bundle (**Marten**)
             Bundle (**Jemmy**)
             Bundle (**Nancy**)
             Bundle (**Seth**)
             Baby (**Maria**)
             Spade (**Seth**)
             Straw (**Seth**)
             Dagger (**Sarah**)
             Maria's shawl (**Seth**)
             Pistol (**Jasper**)

Personal: **Seth:** blindfold
             William: snuff-box, guinea

LIGHTING PLOT

Property fittings required: nil
Exterior. A small green or garden

To open: General overall lighting

No cues

THIS
IS
NOT
THE
END

Lightning Source UK Ltd.
Milton Keynes UK
UKOW01f1837121017

310891UK00005B/404/P